PRIMATES

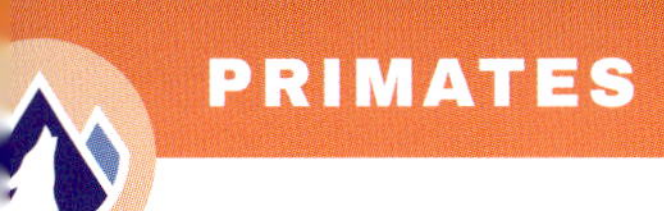

BABOONS

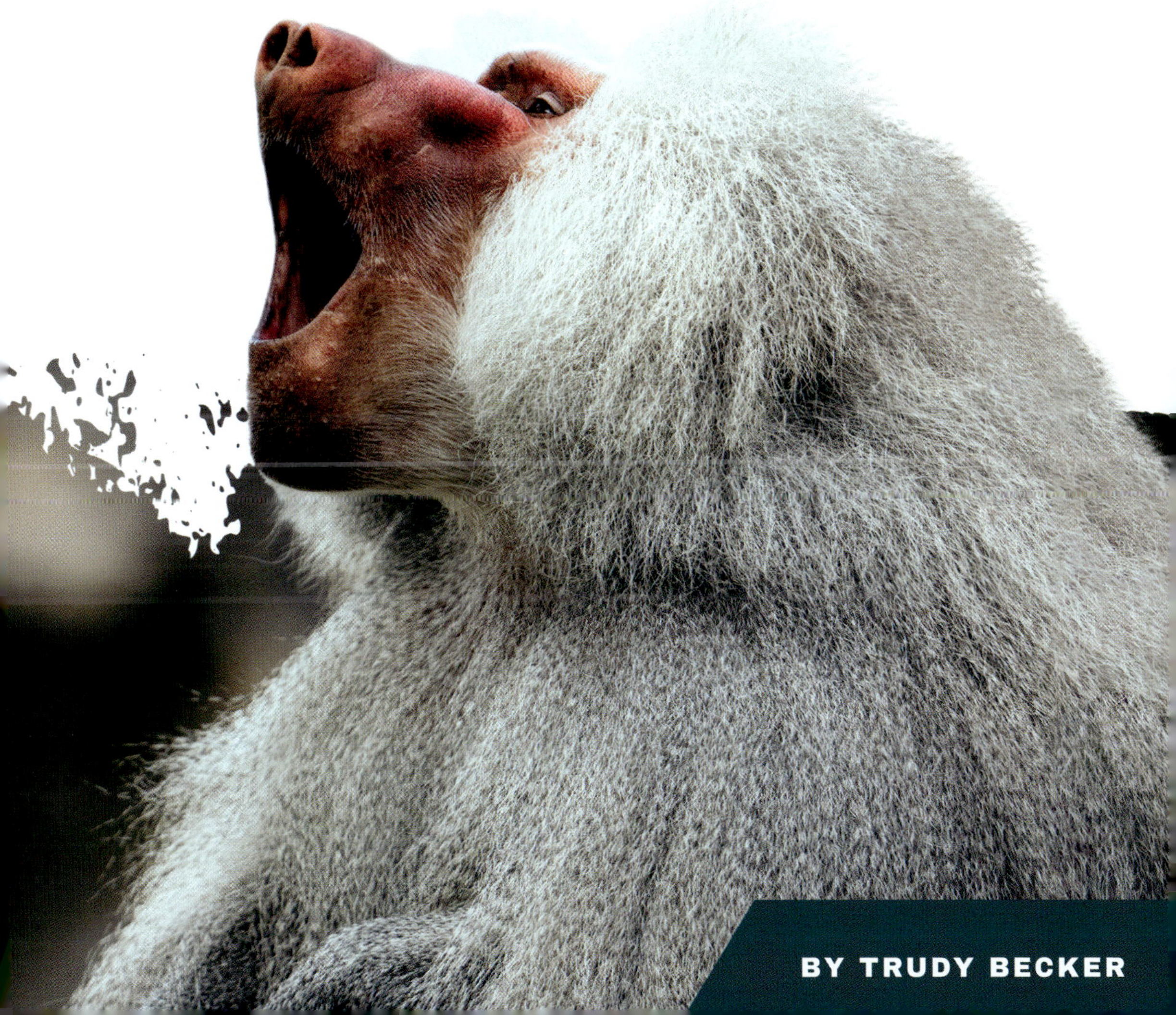

BY TRUDY BECKER

WWW.APEXEDITIONS.COM

Apex is distributed by North Star Editions:
sales@northstareditions.com | 888-417-0195

Produced for Apex by Red Line Editorial.

Photographs ©: Shutterstock Images, cover, 10–11, 12–13, 14, 15, 16–17, 18, 20, 21, 22–23, 24, 25, 26–27, 29; iStockphoto, 1, 4–5, 6, 7, 8–9

Library of Congress Control Number: 2025939158

ISBN
979-8-89250-793-6 (hardcover)
979-8-89250-822-3 (paperback)
979-8-89250-878-0 (ebook pdf)
979-8-89250-851-3 (hosted ebook)

Printed in the United States of America
Mankato, MN
012026

NOTE TO PARENTS AND EDUCATORS

Apex books are designed to build literacy skills in striving readers. Exciting, high-interest content attracts and holds readers' attention. The text is carefully leveled to allow students to achieve success quickly. Additional features, such as bolded glossary words for difficult terms, help build comprehension.

TABLE OF CONTENTS

CHAPTER 1

FIGHTING BACK

A group of baboons rests in the grass. It is a sunny day. Some of the baboons fall asleep. Others **groom** one another.

Baboons often clean bugs and dirt from one another's fur.

A leopard prowls nearby. The big cat creeps toward the baboons. Suddenly, it lunges toward one of them. It bites down hard.

Leopards can leap forward 20 feet (6 m).

Baboons may bark to let others know that danger is near.

STAY AWAY

Baboons face many predators. Lions, cheetahs, and crocodiles may attack them. Baboons often try to scare off predators. They may show their sharp teeth. And they may chase the predators away.

A baboon's sharpest teeth can be close to 2 inches (5 cm) long.

Several other baboons rush at the leopard. They grab its fur. They bite. More baboons join in. Finally, they beat the leopard. It runs away. The baboons are safe.

CHAPTER 2

ALL ABOUT BABOONS

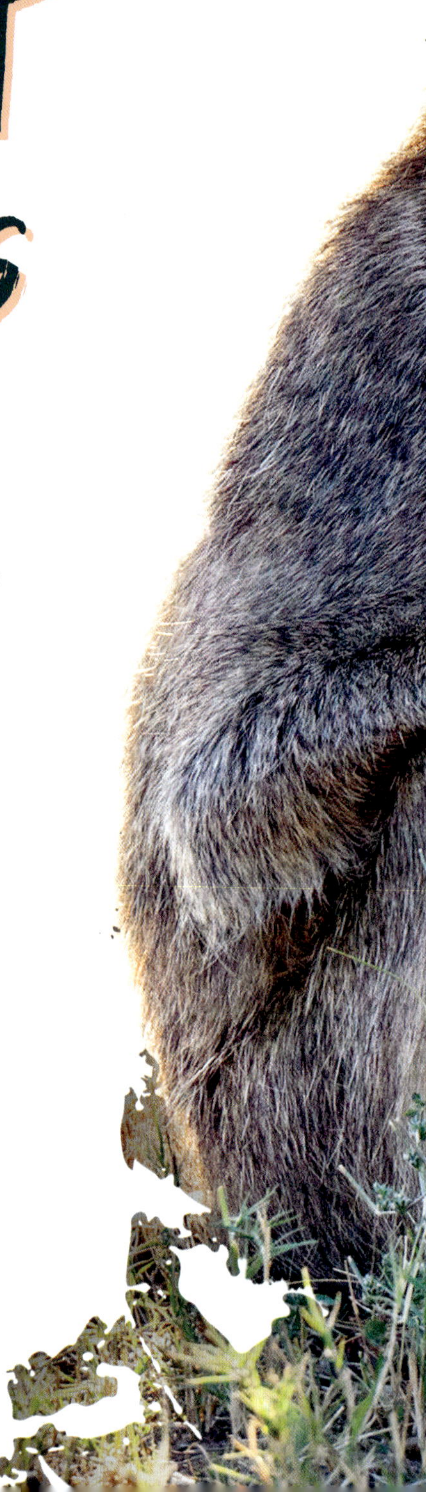

Baboons are some of the world's biggest monkeys. They can weigh more than 80 pounds (36 kg). There are several **species** of baboons. Chacma baboons are the largest.

Male baboons (left) are larger than females.

FAST FACT

Male baboons have extra hair around their necks. The hair is called a "ruff."

Baboons have sharp teeth called canines. Males have extra-long canines.

Baboons have long noses and thick fur. They also have powerful teeth and jaws. That helps them rip food.

Olive baboons live in 25 countries across Africa.

Most baboons live in Africa and Arabia. They usually make homes in dry areas such as **savannas**. Some baboons live in rainforests or mountains.

OLD WORLD

Monkeys are divided into groups based on where they live. One group is old-world monkeys. The other is new-world monkeys. Baboons are old-world monkeys. That means they don't live in the Americas.

Like other old-world monkeys, baboons can't use their tails to grab things.

CHAPTER 3

LIFE IN THE WILD

Baboons are social. They live in groups called troops. A troop usually has around 50 members. The members play together. They also groom and chase one another.

Some troops can have up to 300 baboons.

Baboons get food by **foraging**. They are omnivores. They will eat almost anything. Baboons search for grass, berries, and leaves. Many eat insects. Some also hunt birds and small animals.

Baboons eat many kinds of fruits.

Baboons sleep up high in trees or on cliffs.

In the morning, small groups of baboons go out to look for food. In the afternoon, they take breaks. At night, foraging baboons return home. They sleep with the troop.

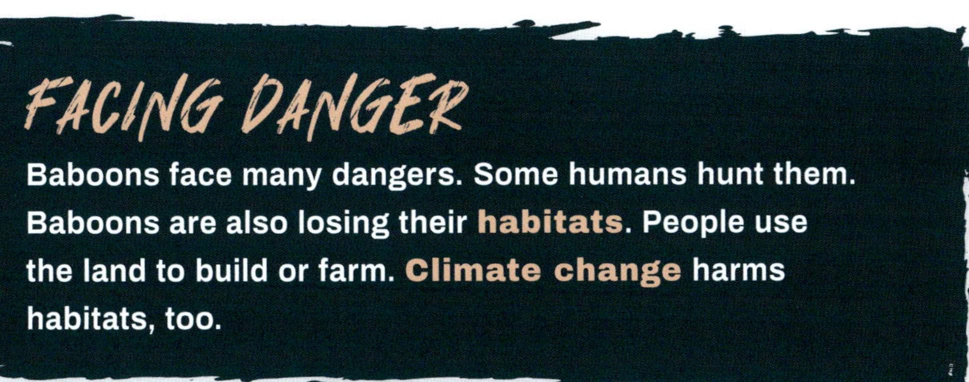

FACING DANGER

Baboons face many dangers. Some humans hunt them. Baboons are also losing their **habitats**. People use the land to build or farm. **Climate change** harms habitats, too.

Climate change can make baboon habitats drier and hotter.

CHAPTER 4

LIFE CYCLE

Baboon troops have a **hierarchy**. Stronger males have more power. The males often fight one another. So, their rankings change.

Baboons may fight over food, mates, or good resting spots.

Baby baboons weigh only a few pounds.

Males compete to mate with females. Females give birth five to six months after mating. A female usually has one baby at a time. She cares for it closely for a year.

RED BOTTOMS

Baboons are known for their red bottoms. The color gets brighter when females are ready to mate. The area puffs up, too. These changes **attract** male baboons.

A baby baboon clings to its mother's fur as she moves around.

FAST FACT
Baboons can live 20 to 30 years in the wild.

Baboons are fully grown after five to eight years. By that time, males have left their troop. They find another troop or form a new one. Females stay with their birth troops.

Full-grown female baboons have babies about every two years.

COMPREHENSION QUESTIONS

Write your answers on a separate piece of paper.

1. Write a few sentences explaining the main idea of Chapter 3.
2. What fact about baboons is most interesting to you? Why?
3. How much can baboons weigh?
   - A. less than 20 pounds (9 kg)
   - B. only 50 pounds (23 kg)
   - C. more than 80 pounds (36 kg)
4. What could happen if a male baboon lost a fight?
   - A. He could get a higher ranking in his troop.
   - B. He could get a lower ranking in his troop.
   - C. He could become the troop's leader.

5. What does **social** mean in this book?

Baboons are ***social****. They live in groups called troops.*

- **A.** spending most of the time alone
- **B.** often spending time with others
- **C.** often awake during the night

6. What does **omnivores** mean in this book?

They are ***omnivores****. They will eat almost anything.*

- **A.** animals that eat only plants
- **B.** animals that eat only meat
- **C.** animals that eat both plants and meat

Answer key on page 32.

GLOSSARY

attract

To make something come closer.

climate change

A dangerous long-term change in Earth's temperature and weather patterns.

foraging

Searching for food.

groom

To clean or care for an animal's fur.

habitats

The places where animals normally live.

hierarchy

A system where members of a group are ranked.

savannas

Flat, grassy areas with few or no trees.

species

Groups of animals or plants that are similar and can breed with one another.

TO LEARN MORE

BOOKS

Huddleston, Emma. *Thank You, Primates*. The Child's World, 2022.

Kenney, Karen Latchana. *Howler Monkeys*. Bellwether Media, 2021.

Rains, Dalton. *Chimpanzees*. Apex Editions, 2025.

ONLINE RESOURCES

Visit **www.apexeditions.com** to find links and resources related to this title.

ABOUT THE AUTHOR

Trudy Becker lives in Minneapolis, Minnesota. She likes exploring new places and loves anything involving books.

INDEX

ANSWER KEY:
1. Answers will vary; 2. Answers will vary; 3. C; 4. B; 5. B; 6. C